# damien rice o

guitar tablature vocal

published 2004

©international music publications ltd
griffin house 161 hammersmith road, london w6 8bs england

arranged and engraved by artemis music ltd. (www.artemismusic.com)

printed in the uk by halstan & co. ltd. (www.halstan.co.uk)

# delicate

**Words and Music by Damien Rice**

with me at all?

*Outro:*

# volcano

Words and Music by Damien Rice

*Intro:*

♩ = 160

Verse:

1. Don't hold your - self_____ like that,
2. Don't throw your - self_____ like that,

*w/light palm muting*

You'll hurt your knees.
In front of me.

I kissed your mouth and back
I kissed your mouth, your back

But that's all I need.
Is that all you need?

*Play 4 times*

Oh,_____ oh.___

Vol - ca - noes___ melt_____ you down.___

___ to you___ you do not need._____ What I am___

She's still too young.___ She's still too___ young.___

___ I___ kissed your___ mouth._____ Oh,_____ oh.___

Vol - ca - noes___ melt_____ you down.___

___ to you___ is not real.___ And what I am___

Still too young.___ She's still too___ young.___

# the blower's daughter

*Words and Music by Damien Rice*

The shor - ter sto - ry.
The col - der wa - ter.

**Gtr 2.** *(2° only)*

Cello arr. for Gtr.

*mp*

No love no glo - ry.
The blo - wer's daugh - ter.

No\_\_\_ he - ro in_____ her\_\_\_ skies.\_\_\_
The\_\_\_ pu - pil in_____ de - nial.\_\_\_

I can't take my eyes\_\_\_

# cannonball

Words and Music by Damien Rice

*Verse*

Gtr. 1

There's still a lit-tle bit of your taste____ in my mouth. There's still a lit-tle bit of you laced____

w/Fig. 1 *(Acous. Gtrs. 2+3)*

____ with my doubt. It's still a lit-tle hard____ to say____ what's go -

— to fall— and I don't want to scare— her. It's not hard to fall and I

**D.C. al Coda**

don't want to lose.— It's not hard to grow— when you know that you just don't know.
*(hold note over)*

### ⊕ *Coda*

# older chests

Words and Music by Damien Rice

♩ = 112

Acous. Gtr. 1

*Pre-chorus:*

*Chorus:*

# amie

Words and Music by Damien Rice

# cheers darlin'

Words and Music by Damien Rice

Cheers,___ dar - lin',      I got your___ wed - ding bells___ in my ear.
Cheers,___ dar - lin',      I got a___ rib - bon of green on my gui - tar.

**Acous. Gtr. 1**

**Acous. Gtr. 2**

*2° only...*
*composite part*

Cheers,___ dar - lin',___ you gave me three cig - ar - rettes to___ smoke my___ tears a - way.
Cheers,___ dar - lin',___ I got a beau - ty queen, to sit not ve - ry far from me.

*Interlude*

# cold water

Words and Music by Damien Rice

# i remember

Words and Music by Damien Rice

'cept you my love.

*Interlude*

Come, all you lost,— dive in - to moss and hope that my san - i - ty co - vers the

*Use T on 6*

# eskimo

Words and Music by Damien Rice

1. Tired - ness

# Prague

**Words and Music by Damien Rice**

all dressed up___ for him___ too.___
all wrapped up___ in him___ too.___

*2nd time Gtrs 2,3+4 play ad lib.*

*Verse:*

Pre - pare my - self___ for a_____ war,
Pre - pare my - self___ for a_____ war,

Elec. Gtr. 1

Elec. Gtr. 4

*mp w/clean tone*          Fig. 1          *end Fig. 1*

Elec. Gtr. 2

*mf w/clean tone*
*Gtr. 3 dbls. ad lib.*

Well, I could wait_____ for you,_____

w/Fig. 2 (Elec. Gtr. 2)
w/Fig. 4 (Elec. Gtr. 3)
w/Fig. 3 (Elec. Gtr. 4)

like that hole_____ in your boot_ wait-ing to be fixed.
What good would that do?_____

_____ but to leave me pricked. Dar-lin',

# silent night

Traditional
Arranged by Lisa Hannigan

# GUITAR TAB GLOSSARY**

## TABLATURE EXPLANATION

**READING TABLATURE:** Tablature illustrates the six strings of the guitar. Notes and chords are indicated by the placement of fret numbers on a given string(s).

*String* ⑥ **3rd** *Fret*   *String* ① **12th** *Fret*   A "C" Chord   "C" Chord Arpeggiated
*String* ③ **13th** *Fret*

## BENDING NOTES

**HALF STEP:** Play the note and bend string one half step.*

**WHOLE STEP:** Play the note and bend string one whole step.

**WHOLE STEP AND A HALF:** Play the note and bend string a whole step and a half.

**QUARTER-TONE BEND:** Play the note and bend string slightly to the equivalent of half a fret.

**PREBEND (Ghost Bend):** Bend to the specified note, before the string is picked.

**PREBEND AND RELEASE:** Bend the string, play it, then release to the original note.

**REVERSE BEND:** Play the already-bent string, then immediately drop it down to the fretted note.

**BEND AND RELEASE:** Play the note and gradually bend to the next pitch, then release to the original note. Only the first note is attacked.

*A half step is the smallest interval in Western music; it is equal to one fret. A whole step equals two frets.

**UNISON BEND:** Play both notes and immediately bend the lower note to the same pitch as the higher note.

**DOUBLE NOTE BEND:** Play both notes and immediately bend both strings simultaneously.

**BENDS INVOLVING MORE THAN ONE STRING:** Play the note and bend string while playing an additional note (or notes) on another string(s). Upon release, relieve pressure from additional note(s), causing original note to sound alone.

**BENDS INVOLVING STATIONARY NOTES:** Play notes and bend lower pitch, then hold until release begins (indicated at the point where line becomes solid).

## TREMOLO BAR

*trem. bar*

**SPECIFIED INTERVAL:** The pitch of a note or chord is lowered to a specified interval and then may or may not return to the original pitch. The activity of the tremolo bar is graphically represented by peaks and valleys.

**UN-SPECIFIED INTERVAL:** The pitch of a note or a chord is lowered to an unspecified interval.

## HARMONICS

harm.   harm.
(8va)

harm.   harm.

**NATURAL HARMONIC:** A finger of the fret hand lightly touches the note or notes indicated in the tab and is played by the pick hand.

A.H.

A.H.

**ARTIFICIAL HARMONIC:** The first tab number is fretted, then the pick hand produces the harmonic by using a finger to lightly touch the same string at the second tab number (in parenthesis) and is then picked by another finger.

(15ma)(8va)(8va)

P.H.   P.H.   P.H.

**ARTIFICIAL "PINCH" HARMONIC:** A note is fretted as indicated by the tab, then the pick hand produces the harmonic by squeezing the pick firmly while using the tip of the index finger in the pick attack. If parenthesis are found around the fretted note, it does not sound. No parenthesis means both the fretted note and A.H. are heard simultaneously.

**By Kenn Chipkin and Aaron Stang

## RHYTHM SLASHES

**STRUM INDICATIONS:** Strum with indicated rhythm. The chord voicings are found on the first page of the transcription underneath the song title.

**SINGLE NOTES IN SLASH NOTATION:** A regular notehead indicates a single note. The circled number below the note indicates which string of the chord to strike. If the note is not in the chord, the fret number will be indicated above the note(s).

**FRETBOARD TAPPING:** "Tap" onto the note indicated by + with a finger of the pick hand, then pull off to the following note held by the fret hand.

**TAP SLIDE:** Same as fretboard tapping, but the tapped note is slid randomly up the fretboard, then pulled off to the following note.

**SHORT GLISSANDO:** Play note for its full value and slide in specified direction at the last possible moment.

**PICK SLIDE:** Slide the edge of the pick in specified direction across the length of the string(s).

**TRILL:** Hammer on and pull off consecutively and as fast as possible between the original note and the grace note.

**ACCENT:** Notes or chords are to be played with added emphasis.

## ARTICULATIONS

**HAMMER ON:** Play lower note, then "hammer on" to higher note with another finger. Only the first note is attacked.

**BEND AND TAP TECHNIQUE:** Play note and bend to specified interval. While holding bend, tap onto note indicated.

**MUTED STRINGS:** A percussive sound is made by laying the fret hand across all six strings while pick hand strikes specified area (low, mid, high strings).

**STACCATO (Detached Notes):** Notes or chords are to be played roughly half their actual value and with separation.

**LEFT HAND HAMMER:** Hammer on the first note played on each string with the left hand.

**LEGATO SLIDE:** Play note and slide to the following note. (Only first note is attacked).

**PALM MUTE:** The note or notes are muted by the palm of the pick hand by lightly touching the string(s) near the bridge.

**DOWN STROKES AND UPSTROKES:** Notes or chords are to be played with either a downstroke (■) or upstroke (v) of the pick.

**PULL OFF:** Play higher note, then "pull off" to lower note with another finger. Only the first note is attacked.

**LONG GLISSANDO:** Play note and slide in specified direction for the full value of the note.

**TREMOLO PICKING:** The note or notes are picked as fast as possible.

**VIBRATO:** The pitch of a note is varied by a rapid shaking of the fret hand finger, wrist, and forearm.